EASY INDIAN POT COOKBOOK

HEALING WITH SPICES AND HERBS

50 INSTANT POT RECIPES

JOSEPH VEEBE

Copyright © 2019 by Joseph Veebe. All Rights Reserved.

No part of this publication may be reproduced, distributed, or transmitted in any form or by any means, including photocopying, recording, or other electronic or mechanical methods, or by any information storage and retrieval system without the prior written permission of the publisher, except in the case of very brief quotations embodied in critical reviews and certain other noncommercial uses permitted by copyright law.

Books in this Series:

TABLE OF CONTENTS

CHAPTER 1. INTRODUCTION

INTRODUCTION

This book is an attempt to share my experience cooking with my instant pot which has become the most essential kitchen appliance in my home. The focus is still healthy cooking and eating like all my other books. Instant pot enables you to cook healthy meals even faster! While most of the recipes here are Indian, if you are looking for an authentic Indian recipe book, this is NOT it. The goal is to get 100% healthy dishes (healthy and fresh ingredients, avoid non-healthy fats and processed ingredients) with at least 80% of Indian taste and flavor with at most 20% effort of traditional Indian recipes! While included fifty recipe ideas may not seem like a whole lot, there are tips and tricks described to try your own variations and apply your creativity to cook even more dishes.

While I love to cook healthy meals for my family, I do not like to spend too much time in the kitchen nor following prescription recipes. I like to the cooking process to be fast, easy and creative. I hope you will use the recipe ideas given in this book and create your own healthy and tasty dishes.

INSTANT POT OR ELECTRIC PROGRAMMABLE PRESSURE COOKER

Instant Pot is essentially an electric or electronic pressure cooker. A pressure cooker is a cooking device that can cook food by sealing the contents that are being cooked to retain high steam pressure inside. At higher pressure, the boiling temperature of water rises, and the food is cooked at a much higher temperature compared to open stovetop cooking where the temperature remains constant at 100 degrees centigrade (or 212 degrees Fahrenheit). Most often the result of retaining high pressure helps the food to cook much faster, retain the nutrition from escaping, and reduce the cooking time significantly. Some foods, especially dried foods such as beans, lentils typically take very long to cook on the open stove top. Meat also usually takes more time to cook on the stovetop.

My mother always used a manual pressure cooker for cooking lentils and meats such as beef or pork. Depending on the type of food cooked, she used to count the "whistles" or steam release sounds to determine the cooking is done depending on what is being cooked. While cooking was indeed faster, it needed some level of babysitting to make sure the food is not overcooked. These cookers were designed to be used on the stovetop, so heating needed to be manually regulated. Also, there used to be a safety issue of blowing up the cooker, the lid, or the safety valve.

The electric pressure cooker or instant pot fix all those drawbacks and provide many other features that make instant pot one of the most invaluable cooking tools in the market today.

While there is a brand of programmable electric pressure cooker under the name Instant Pot, in this book Instant Pot refers to any programmable electric pressure cooker from a number of manufacturers. I use a Rosewill Home 6-liter electric cooker. I purchased this a couple of years ago because it was inexpensive compared to others and provided similar features as the expensive ones. This one does not have a yogurt setting or timed steam release feature. This has been one of the most used devices in my kitchen for the past several years.

The electric pressure cooker has a pressure-cooking container, an inner pot or an insert for holding food and a lid with pressure sealing valve. The pressure-cooking container is sort of high tech with pressure and temperature sensors, a microprocessor (or computer) that can control and regulate the temperature and pressure based on the food being cooked and allows the user to program the cooking function.

Most electric pressure cookers or instant pots offer the following capabilities:

1. Automatic settings for cooking most common food items such as:
   - Meat
   - Poultry
   - White Rice
   - Brown Rice
   - Beans
   - Steam
   - Soup
   - Slow cook
   - Saute
   - Vegetables
   - Curry

- Multi-grain
- Chili
- Congee/Porridge
- Yogurt

2. Manual mode

Manual mode allows one to set both cooking pressure and cooking time to the desired level depending on the food or cooking needs. Some of you may be familiar with cameras that have both automatic and manual modes. Similar to a camera, the manual mode allows fine control and is usually for a more experienced user. Manual mode is especially useful in cooking the food over a long time such as overnight or over many hours. The manual pressure mode allows the following:

- Low pressure (typically 5-7 psi)
- Medium pressure (10-12 psi)
- High pressure (15 psi)

3. Safety

An electric pressure cooker has more safety features built into it than a manual pressure cooker. An electric pressure cooker has the ability to regulate the power or heat and can shut off automatically, so the pressure is maintained at the set level and cooking is done for the set amount of time. Therefore, the risk of blowing the safety valve or pressure release mechanism is much lower compared to a manual pressure cooker.

4. Set it and forget it

Unlike a manual pressure cooker, the instant pot does not need intervention from the user once it is set correctly for the food that is being cooked. The cooker will regulate the power or heat and can shut off automatically, so the pressure is maintained at the set level and cooking is done for the set amount of time. Whether you are using automatic functions or manual settings, the instant pot allows one to set the cooker and go to work and come back to warm food or set the cooker and go to a shower or shopping with the knowledge that the food will be cooked, and the cooker will be automatically turned off after it is done. Most cookers also have a delay timer so the cooking can start at the desired time.

5. Intelligent programming

As the instant pot is a sophisticated device with sensors and an onboard computer (microprocessor), it is no surprise that the instant pot is programmable.
The microprocessor monitors pressure, temperature, and cooking time. It can adjust the intensity of heating and duration based on the type of food being prepared.

6. Smart Cooker with Wifi connectivity and app-controlled

Some instant pots, which are considered to be the 4th generation pressure cookers have built-in wifi capability to be operated and controlled through the internet or wifi with much easier interfaces through apps running on your mobile or computer device. With such instant pots, one can start/stop or change cooking modes remotely (from work for example) through a mobile phone interface.

There are many benefits that make the instant pot as one of the must-haves in any kitchen:

1. Save time & energy

Under very high pressure, the water boils at higher than the usual 100-degree centigrade (212-degree Fahrenheit) resulting in faster cooking at a higher consistent temperature. In ordinary stovetop cooking, the temperature stays at the boiling point of water and as a result, more time is required for cooking. On an average, electric pressure cooker cuts down the cooking time at least half in most cases.

The electric pressure cooker inner pot is highly insulated from outside so it is much more efficient and does not loose heating energy compared to a stovetop manual cooker where the heat is lost to surroundings.

Since the cooker is highly sealed to preserve steam, much less water is required for cooking. This, once again, reduces cooking time and saves energy.

2. Preserve nutrients

Open boiling for long periods of time can result in the loss of water-soluble nutrients in the food. Sealed pressure cooking not only retains the nutrients but also cooks quickly and evenly resulting in retaining more nutrients than conventional cooking.

3. Safety

Sometimes, there is a concern about the cooker under pressure exploding. But this does not happen in reality. Modern electric pressure cookers are not only built very sturdy but also has sensors that regulate the amount of heat and pressure. Since these cookers automatically shut off once the cooking is over, they can cook unattended. With a conventional pressure cooker, stovetop cooking can cause fire and overcooking. With an electric cooker, you don't have to worry wondering if you forgot to switch off the stove while leaving home in a hurry. Believe me, it happens too often and until I started using an instant pot, this was always a worry for me.

4. Automatic function

Automatic functions let you select the food using the push-button panel on the cooker and have the cooker automatically adjust pressure and cooking time. The manual setting allows you to cook for a long duration (slow cook or simmer broths) as well as give you the control to cook at the pressure and duration you like.

5. Kill microorganisms and neutralizing toxins

Since the cooking temperature is much higher than the usual boiling point of water, many of the microorganisms are easily and quickly neutralized.

Mold-based toxins in food grains such as rice, wheat, corn, and beans can happen as a result of exposure to humidity. Pressure cooking can neutralize such toxins.

Pressure cooking is also known to neutralize toxins in kidney beans and prevent poisoning.

In addition to all these benefits, there are many other reasons why I decided to buy an instant pot:

1. Cooks beans, lentils, and chickpeas superfast. Especially, this is great if you are trying to balance protein in your food through lentils instead of consuming meat or diaries all the time.
2. Since I cook rice (brown rice mostly), I don't need a separate rice cooker as the instant pot can do it in a jiffy, especially brown rice which may take more time in a traditional rice cooker.
3. I make steamed rice cakes often. This is a perfect device for steaming anything superfast – including veggies and fish.
4. Though I am repeating this, the timer function is extremely convenient. It is like set it and forget it. The food is automatically made.
5. The other big thing about instant pot is that it can sauté and cook in the same pot. One does not have to cook and sauté in separate pans. In one pot you can sauté your onions, herbs, and spices and then add the food you want to cook and let it do its magic.

6. Once again, the multiple functions of the instant pot help to replace several devices such as rice cooker, steamer, pressure cooker and slow cooker (and in some cases yogurt maker as well)– all these functions can be done by instant pot much more efficiently.

7. Cleaning – Cleaning the inner pot and the lid is simple and straight forward.

CHAPTER 2. TIPS FOR COOKING INDIAN FOOD IN INSTANT POT

GENERAL TIPS FOR COOKING IN ONE POT

The instant pot is generally a sophisticated cooking device. There are many available on the market offering mostly similar functions. Below are some of the tips for cooking using Instant Pot.

1. The pressure cooker is fundamentally based on steam pressure. That means there needs to be some water in the inner pot for it to build steam. For foods that do not expand when cooked – e.g. chicken, vegetables, etc. recommendation is to add 1/2 – 1 cup of water. For foods that expand such as beans, rice, etc. follow the recommended measure of water, broth, or other fluids.

2. Use different cooking modes as necessary while cooking. For example, I use sauté function all the time to sauté onions and spices before meat or vegetables are added to the cooker. Once saluted, the cooker mode could be changed to vegetable, chicken, or meat and close the lid to let the cooker do its trick.

3. Adjust the temperature
   Some instant pot allows you to adjust sauté temperature to high, medium, and low. This gives you some level of control during sautéing

4. Adjust pressure

Adjusting cooking pressure using manual mode allows you to set the pressure level to low, medium or high

5. Study how your cooker works in the manual cooking mode. Some electric pressure cookers count down the cooking time after achieving the desired pressure. But some may count down from the start. When using such cookers, add 10-15 minutes to the cooking time for manual cooking so as to build up the pressure.

6. Get a second insert and any accessories for your needs

    The instant pot comes with an inner pot that is used for cooking food. Some are steel pots and some with non-stick coating. I use the non-stick one when I need to sauté before pressure cook. The steel one is good for making soups and beans etc. In any case, having multiple pots allow you to cook multiple dishes in one cooking session without having to transfer food and clean one insert.

    Some of the other accessories such as steaming racks are good if you plan to use steam function more often for making steam cakes or steaming veggies.

7. Keep extra sealing rings handy

    You may want to keep a couple of extra sealing rings for many reasons. One, sealing ring, after extensive use could become leaky and can let steam escape, second, more important reason is to have separate sealing rings for the preparation savory, spicy, and sweet dishes as the sealing ring can retain the smell and taste of the previously cooked items.

8. Be prepared for too watery food
    Since the instant pot traps all the steam and water content, even if you have not poured much water, at the end of cooking you may find a more watery dish than you intend for. One tip is to understand which food items have high water content and which one does not. For example, if you are cooking fresh meat (chicken, beef, or pork) or vegetables, you may want to pour less water or other liquid than you would do on the stovetop. In some cases when I cook chicken, I hardly pour any water as chicken already retains some amount of water.
    In case your dish ends up having too much water than you intended, you can add a couple of tablespoons of cornstarch at the *end of cook*ing to make the food thicken.
9. Cooking with milk
    Many instant pots have a yogurt making function which works really great if you like making your own yogurt instead of buying from the store. However, besides yogurt making, cooking milk-based food can be tricky in an instead pot. Milk can easily scald or curdle if cooked in the instant pot. If you must add milk or dairy ingredients to your dish being cooked in the instant pot, wait to add them until the pressure-cooking process is complete.
10. You can cook food directly from the freezer in the instant pot. There is no need to thaw the food prior to cooking to as required in the case of other cooking devices to ensure uniform cooking. Since instant pot can maintain a very high temperature

inside, frozen food, typically, will get thawed very quickly.

11. Allow extra time when cooking frozen items. As you will need to account for thawing the food, allowing 2-3 minutes extra time for frozen food will ensure the thawing process is accounted for.

12. Remember that while soaking does reduce cooking times, instant pot can cook beans, chickpeas, and lentils without soaking. While I recommend prior soaking of beans and lentils, the high temperature in the instant pot allows cooking these items without soaking and still cook in less time than on a stovetop with pre-soaked food.

13. Delay timer is a great feature that allows cooking to start at a set time delay. This function is extremely useful when you the food to be cooked just prior to you are ready to eat but the prep is done much earlier such as just before leaving home in the morning for office work or before going shopping, or for a walk, etc.

14. Get familiar with the valve positioning and pressure release. The valve in the open position is used for steaming vegetables or making steam cakes for steamed food. The valve in the sealing position is used when you want to pressure cook your food. When cooking in pressure cooking mode with the valve in the sealing position, the pressure will need to be released after the cooking is done. The two pressure release modes are called natural pressure release or quick pressure release.

15. In the natural pressure release, the valve remains sealed until the pressure is released naturally as a result of the cooker cooling down and the steam inside the cooker condenses. The float valve will drop at the end of the natural pressure release and you will be able to open the lid even with the pressure valve in sealing position. Natural pressure release could take anywhere between 5 to 30 minutes depending on the amount of food you are cooking, how full the cooker is etc. Since the food continues to get cooked during natural pressure release, this mode is used when there is no risk of overcooking the food such as meat dishes, soups, broths, lentils, etc.

16. In quick pressure release, the pressure sealing valve is moved from a sealing position to open position. All the steam escapes through the valve in 5-10 seconds and float valve drops indicating the end of cooking. You can open the lid as soon as the float valve drops. This mode is used when you are cooking food that requires very short cook times such as fish, vegetables, etc. By releasing the pressure quickly, we make sure the food is not overcooked.

A Cooking time conversion chart is given in the Appendix. This is a very convenient chart for cooking a wide variety of food items. These cooking times approximations and should, largely, work for most electric pressure cookers.

GENERAL TIPS FOR COOKING WITH SPICES

Since this book is about using instant pot to cook Indian food, some general tips and recommendations on cooking and using spices are included. When used in cooking, spices and herbs broadly provide the many benefits.

- Color your food and make it attractive to eat
- Provide flavor and taste to the food without adding unhealthy components like salt and fat
- Transforms even ordinary/common food into tasty dishes saving money
- Spices and herbs make the cooked food healthier by preventing the formation of harmful compounds during cooking
- Spices and herbs are a very good source of micro-nutrients such as anti-oxidants, anti-inflammatory compounds, vitamins and minerals
- Stimulates appetite, improve digestion and help maintain a healthy intestine which in turn improves immunity and general health
- Protects from many health conditions such as cancer, diabetes, and cholesterol, etc.
- Helps in reversing some diseases
- Boosts brain function and slow down the aging process

Please see my other books on spices and herbs for detailed discussion on health benefits of spices and herbs.

Below are the suggestions when you are starting out cooking with and using spices and herbs:

1. Test if you can tolerate a specific spice

Test out spices to determine if you are allergic to any of the spices or you simply don't like any. This can be done by trying out these spices in small amounts either in cooking or in drinks. You may be allergic to some spices and it can cause serious issues. Once, a friend of mine offered masala chai (spiced tea) to his landlord only to have him a serious reaction and had to call emergency medical services.

2. Try out spices individually first before trying various spice blends

Individual spices offer many benefits and also can be simple to use when are starting out experimenting with spices. Ginger and garlic may be used with any meat dish. Turmeric similarly can be used while sautéing onions and can color your vegetables and make it more palatable.

3. Start with the mild spices or spices you have already been exposed to. I recommend the following order:

    a. Cinnamon. You might already have been using this and is ok as part of desserts or baked foods
    b. Black Pepper. Black pepper is also part of some of the common foods that you eat on a daily basis including soups, pasta, burgers, etc.
    c. Chili powder
    d. Turmeric powder

    e. Coriander Powder
    f. Cumin
    g. Fennel
    h. Other Spices

The reason for this suggested order is for you to start with some of the spices you may already have been exposed to through some of the common foods or sauces available in restaurants or frozen, prepared food from supermarkets.

4. Do you need to temper the spice mix?

Tempering, blooming or gently frying spices achieves the following:

    a. It reduces the pungent or raw taste of the spices
    b. It deepens flavor
    c. It helps the body in easy absorption of the micro-nutrients in the spices. For example, curcumin in turmeric is not easily absorbed. But tempering them in oil makes it much easier for the body to absorb.
    d. Tempering is required/recommended for pungent spices such as chili, coriander, cumin, etc. but spices like cardamom, cinnamon, nutmeg, and ginger may be used directly such as done in spice tea or baking

5. How to temper or fry spices

Method 1:

a. Add 2-3 teaspoons of butter, vegetable oil, coconut oil, or olive oil to a sauté pan or instant pot set in sauté mode. Make sure the heat is set to medium so as not to burn the spice

b. Test out the heat of the pan by dropping a bit of spice. If it bubbles up and simmers the pan is ready. If not, turn up the heat a bit more

c. Add the spices all together and stir well so it is coated with oil. Stir for a minute so the spices are fried, and aroma is released. Now you can add vegetables or meat and cook.

Method 2: Tempering spice with onions, garlic and/ or ginger

d. Add 2-3 teaspoons of butter, vegetable oil, coconut oil or olive oil, to a sauté pan or instant pot set in sauté mode.

e. Add onions (and ginger and garlic), stir well until onions turn translucent

f. Add the spices all together and stir well so it is coated with oil. Stir for a minute so the spices are fried, and aroma is released. Now you can add vegetables or meat and cook.

Method 3: Tempering spice paste

An alternative way to fry spice is to make it a paste first and then fry it in oil as described in 6. The easy way to make the spice mix into a paste is to add one tablespoon or enough water to spice and mix it to make a past.

You will be using one or more of the spices listed above and will be using instant pot's sautéing function to temper spices while cooking many of the recipes listed later in this book.

CHAPTER 3. COOKING RICE DISHES

Rice and other grains expand when cooked will need to have sufficient water for them to cook properly. The typical ratio of rice to water in the instant pot is 1:1, which means 1 cup water for each cup of rice. This ratio is lower than other rice cookers simply because instant pot retains water while cooking while other cookers lose some of the water and therefore need a higher ratio (1:1.25-1.5) of water. Depending on the type of rice used, the cooking time also varies. Brown rice typically takes a long time (20-25 minutes) to cook compared to Jasmin or basmati rice (4-5 minutes). Soaking brown rice reduces cooking time somewhat but not significantly. Brown rice also may require a bit higher ratio of rice to water (this author recommends 1:1.25 for brown rice).

If you are cooking vegetables or fish with rice, make sure to use white rice which has comparable cooking time. Brown rice may be with beef or other meat which takes more time to cook.

While general guideline of rice to water ratio of 1:1 or 1:1.25 is recommended, you may increase or decrease the water ratio slightly depending on the following:
- Types of rice used
- Personal taste, how soft you like the cooked rice
- Other ingredients cooked with rice such as tomatoes, peas, green beans, carrot, etc. These may actually generate some water while cooking and therefore adjust water accordingly.
- If you are making pilaf or biriyani and are using butter or other oil as part of cooking, you want the rice to be not fully cooked and sticky instead remain

separate from the ingredients. In that case, you may use a little bit lower ratio than rice is cooked alone.

RICE PILAF AND SALMON

Ingredients

- 2 4 oz wild-caught frozen salmon filets
- ½ cup of basmati rice
- 1 cup of bone broth/any broth or water
- ¼ cup dried vegetable seasoning/blend
- 2 tbsp butter or 2 tbsp olive oil
- ¼ cup green onions chopped
- ¼ tsp turmeric
- ¼ tsp paprika
- ¼ tsp salt or to taste
- ¼ tsp black pepper powder

Method

1. Instant pot set to sauté, add butter or olive oil. Sauté onions and add paprika and turmeric. Now add bone broth, vegetable mix/seasoning, and soaked rice and a pinch of salt.
2. Insert steamer rack on top and arrange frozen salmon filets seasoned with salt and pepper
3. Pressure cook for 6 minutes. Release pressure quickly

Recipe Note: Basmati rice may be replaced with Brown rice. brown rice usually takes around 20 minutes compared to Jasmin or basmati rice which takes only about 5 minutes. Soaking brown rice for an hour reduces the cooking time to half or less.

PARMESAN RICE WITH SHRIMP

Ingredients

- 1lb uncooked medium shrimp, peeled and deveined
- 2 cup of basmati rice
- 2 cups bone broth/any broth or water
- 2 tbsp olive oil
- 1 tsp grated ginger
- 2 tsp minced garlic
- ½ cup green onions chopped
- ¼ tsp salt or to taste
- ¼ tsp black pepper powder
- ¼ cup parsley chopped or 2 tbsp dried parsley flakes
- ½ cup grated parmesan cheese

Method

1. Instant pot set to sauté, add olive oil. Sauté green onions, garlic, ginger. Now add shrimp and sauté for 1 minute. Now add bone broth and soaked rice and salt.
2. Pressure cook high for 7 minutes or select white rice on the instant pot. Release pressure quickly
3. Open the instant pot. Add lime juice parsley and cheese while rice is hot. Mix well and serve.

Recipe Note: Basmati rice may be replaced with Brown rice. brown rice usually takes around 20 minutes compared to Jasmin or basmati rice which takes only about 5 minutes. Soaking brown rice for an hour reduces the cooking time to half or less.

SHRIMP FRIED RICE

Ingredients

- 1lb uncooked medium shrimp, peeled and deveined
- 2 cup of basmati rice
- 2 cups of bone broth/any broth or water
- 2 tbsp olive oil
- 1 tsp grated ginger
- 2 tsp minced garlic
- ½ cup green onions chopped
- ¼ tsp salt or to taste
- ¼ tsp black pepper powder
- ¼ cup parsley chopped or 2 tbsp dried parsley flakes
- ½ cup grated parmesan cheese

Method

1. Instant pot set to saute, add olive oil. Saute green onions, garlic, ginger. Now add shrimp and saute for 1 minute . Now add bone broth rice and salt.
2. Pressure cook high for 7 minutes or select white rice on the instant pot. Release pressure quickly
3. Open the instant pot. Add lime juice parsley and cheese while rice is hot. Mix well and serve.

WHITE OR BROWN RICE

Ingredients

- 1 cup of rice
- 1 – 1.5 cups of water
- 1 tsp olive oil or butter
- Salt to taste

Method

1. Wash rice in cold running water
2. Add rice to the instant pot, add oil or butter and water
3. Set the instant pot to white rice or brown rice depending on the type of rice used
4. Close the lid and set the valve to the sealing position.
5. Once the rice is cooked, let it sit for 10 minutes and release the rest of the steam manually
6. Serve with curry or any of the other dishes described in this book.

Notes:

1. White rice usually takes less cooking time than brown or wild rice. Typically, brown rice takes about twice the time as white rice and wild rice takes about 3 times as white rice
2. If you are using brown rice or wild rice, use 1.5 cups of water to 1 cup rice. White rice may be cooked 1 cup of water for each cup of rice.
3. If your instant pot does have only one rice setting (instead of separate settings for white and brown), this setting is typically for white rice. For brown rice, use manual setting and use about 20-22 minutes and for wild or black rice about 30 minutes

TOMATO RICE

This is a good way to color your rice and also include turmeric, ginger, and garlic as part of the diet. The traditional way to make this is more elaborate. However, this recipe is an easy instant pot version.

Basic Ingredients

- 2 cup basmati rice washed
- 2-1/2 cups of water
- 1 tsp turmeric powder
- 2 tsp oil
- 1 pinch black pepper powder
- 4 medium tomato chopped
- 1 medium onion chopped
- Salt to taste
- ¼ cup cilantro chopped
- 3 cloves of garlic crushed
- ½ inch piece of ginger, thinly sliced

Optional Ingredients

- ½ tsp mustard seeds
- ½ cumin seeds
- 1-2 jalapenos sliced, and seeds removed

Method

1. Set instant pot to sauté. Add oil and crackle optional mustard and cumin seeds

2. Add onions, garlic, ginger, and optional jalapenos; sauté until onions are golden brown.

3. Add turmeric and pepper and mix. Now add the tomatoes; mix well for a couple of minutes.

4. Now add the rice. Add 2-1/2 cups of water. Mix. Close and cook on white rice setting.

5. Once the rice is cooked and steam is released naturally, open the lid, add chopped cilantro, salt to taste, and mix well. Serve hot.

Recipe Notes:

1. Instead of white rice, brown rice may be used. If you are using brown rice, add ½ cup more water and cook in the brown rice setting.

2. To give the rice a little more heat, use more Jalapenos or use Jalapenos with the seeds (which holds the heat).

YELLOW RICE WITH PEAS

This is another easy rice dish that can be quickly made in the instant pot. The yellow color is coming from turmeric, which is one of the healthy spices I have extensively used in the recipes.

Basic Ingredients

- 2 cups of basmati rice washed and soaked for 10 minutes
- 2-1/2 cups of clear bone broth, vegetable or chicken broth

- 1 tsp turmeric powder
- 2 tsp olive or coconut oil
- 1 pinch black pepper powder
- 2 cups of frozen peas
- 1 medium onion chopped
- ¼ tsp salt
- ¼ cup cilantro chopped
- 3 cloves of garlic crushed
- ½ inch piece of ginger, thinly sliced

Optional Ingredients

- ½ tsp mustard seeds
- ½ cumin seeds
- 1-2 jalapenos sliced, and seeds removed

Method

1. Set instant pot to sauté. Add oil and crackle optional mustard and cumin seeds
2. Add onions, garlic, ginger, and optional jalapenos; sauté until onions are golden brown.
3. Add turmeric and pepper and mix. Now add the peas; mix well for a couple of minutes.
4. Now add the rice. Saute for a minute. Add broth and salt. Mix. Close and cook on white rice setting with valve in sealing position.
5. Once the rice is cooked and steam is released naturally, open the lid, add chopped cilantro, salt to taste, and mix well. Serve hot.

Recipe Notes:

1. Instead of white rice, brown rice may be used. If you are using brown rice, add ½ cup more water and cook in brown rice setting.
2. To give the rice a little more heat, use more Jalapenos or use Jalapenos with the seeds (which holds the heat).
3. If you are using manual setting. Set the instant pot to high pressure and 5 minutes (for white rice) and about 12-15 minutes for brown rice

PEAS PILAF

This is another easy rice dish that can be quickly made in the instant pot.

Ingredients

- 2 cups of basmati rice washed and soaked for 10 minutes
- 2-1/2 cups of clear bone broth, vegetable or chicken broth
- 2 tsp butter
- 1-1/2 cups of frozen peas
- 1 medium onion chopped
- 1 green chili chopped
- Salt to taste
- ½ cup cilantro chopped
- ½ cup mint leaves
- 3 cloves of garlic crushed
- ½ inch piece of ginger, thinly sliced

Whole Spices

- 1 inch cinnamon
- 4 cloves
- 4 green cardamom
- 1-2 bay leaf
- 1 tsp cumin

Method

1. Set instant pot to sauté. Add butter and sauté the whole spices for about 30 seconds to 1 minute
2. Add onions, garlic, ginger, and chili; sauté until onions are golden brown.
3. Add the peas; mix well for a couple of minutes.
4. Now add the rice, mint, and cilantro. Saute for a minute. Add broth and salt. Mix. Close and cook on white rice setting with valve in sealing position.
5. Once the rice is cooked and steam is released naturally, open the lid. mix well. Serve hot.

Recipe Notes:

1. Instead of white rice, brown rice may be used. If you are using brown rice, add ½ cup more water and cook in the brown rice setting.
2. If you are using the manual setting, set the instant pot to high pressure and 5 minutes (for white rice) and about 12-15 minutes for brown rice

JEERA OR CUMIN RICE

Jeera or cumin rice is another one of Indian dishes and easy to make.

Basic Ingredients

- 2 cups basmati rice washed and soaked for 10 minutes
- 2-1/2 cups clear bone broth, vegetable or chicken broth
- 2 tsp olive or coconut oil
- 1 tsp cumin seeds
- 3-4 cloves
- 1 bay leaf
- 1 inch cinnamon stick
- ¼ tsp salt
- ¼ cup cilantro chopped
- 1-2 jalapenos chopped finely, and seeds removed

Method

1. Set instant pot to sauté. Add oil and crackle cumin seeds.
2. Add onions, garlic, ginger, and optional jalapenos; sauté until onions are golden brown.
3. Add turmeric and pepper and mix. Now add the peas; mix well for a couple of minutes.
4. Now add the rice. Sauté for a minute. Add broth and salt. Mix. Close and cook on white rice setting with valve in sealing position.
5. Once the rice is cooked and steam is released naturally, open the lid, add chopped cilantro, salt to taste, and mix well. Serve hot.

COCONUT RICE

Coconut has many health benefits including antioxidant and anti-inflammatory benefits. This recipe is simple and easy to make.

Basic Ingredients

- 2 cups basmati rice washed and soaked for 10 minutes
- 1 can of 15 oz coconut milk
- 2 tbsp olive oil
- 1 bay leaf
- 2-3 crushed cardamoms
- 1 tbsp grated coconut (optional)
- 1 cup of water

Method

1. Set instant pot to sauté. Add oil and toast cardamoms, bay leaf and optional grated coconut for 1 minute.
2. Now add the rice. Sauté for 1-2 minutes. Add coconut milk, water, and salt. Mix. Close and cook on white rice setting with valve in sealing position.
3. Once the rice is cooked and steam is released naturally, open the lid use a fork to fluff the rice, and serve with lentils or other curries.

COCONUT CHICKEN CURRY RICE

Coconut has many health benefits including antioxidant and anti-inflammatory benefits.

Basic Ingredients

- 1 cups basmati rice washed
- 1.5 cup frozen peas + chopped carrots
- 1 can of 15 oz coconut milk
- 2 tbsp olive oil
- 1 bay leaf
- 2-3 crushed cardamoms
- 2-3 cloves
- 2 tsp ginger garlic paste
- 1 lb chicken (drumsticks or thighs)
- 2 tbsp grated coconut (optional)
- 2 tsp curry powder
- 1 cup water

Method

1. Set instant pot to sauté. Add oil and toast cardamoms, cloves, bay leaf and optional grated coconut for 1 minute.
2. Now add curry powder and mix well. the rice. Sauté for 1-2 minutes. Add vegetables and sauté for 10 minutes or until vegetables are softened. Add coconut milk, water and salt. Mix. Stir in rice and chicken. Close and cook on white rice setting with valve in sealing position.

3. Once the rice is cooked and steam is released naturally, open the lid use a fork to fluff the rice, and serve with lentils or other curries.

MIXED VEGETABLE RICE

Basic Ingredients

- 2 cups basmati rice washed and soaked for 10 minutes
- 2-1/2 cups clear broth, vegetable or chicken bone broth
- 1 tsp turmeric powder
- 1 inch cinnamon piece
- 4 cardamoms
- 2 tsp butter
- 1 pinch black pepper powder
- ¼ cup of frozen peas
- ½ cup carrot sliced
- ¾ cup cabbage chopped
- ½ cup cauliflower chopped
- 1 medium onion chopped
- ¼ tsp salt
- ¼ cup cilantro chopped
- 3 cloves of garlic crushed
- ½ inch piece of ginger, thinly sliced

Optional Ingredients

- ½ tsp mustard seeds
- ½ cumin seeds

- 1-2 jalapenos sliced, and seeds removed
- 2 tbsp grated coconut

Method

1. Set instant pot to sauté. Add oil and crackle optional mustard and cumin seeds
2. Add onions, garlic, ginger and optional jalapenos; sauté until onions are golden brown.
3. Add turmeric and pepper and mix. Now add the peas; mix well for a couple of minutes.
4. Now add the rice. Sauté for a minute. Add broth and salt. Mix. Close and cook on white rice setting with valve in sealing position.
5. Once the rice is cooked and steam is released naturally, open the lid, add chopped cilantro, salt to taste and mix well. Serve hot.

Recipe Notes:

1. Instead of white rice, brown rice may be used. If you are using brown rice, add ½ cup more water and cook in the brown rice setting.
2. To give the rice a little more heat, use more Jalapenos or use Jalapenos with the seeds (which holds the heat).
3. If you are using the manual setting, set the instant pot to high pressure and 5 minutes (for white rice) and about 12-15 minutes for brown rice

CHAPTER 4. COOKING FISH AND SEAFOOD

Fish and seafood typically take much less time to cook than other foods. Fish filet, shrimp and lobster take about 2-3 minutes while whole fish 5-6 minutes, While I have given about 5 minutes in the following recipes, you may want to adjust it depending on the level of cooking and your personal preference.

BAKED SALMON WITH LIME SAUCE

Ingredients

- 2 4 oz wild-caught frozen salmon fillets
For sauce
- 1 tsp olive oil or butter
- Salt to taste
- 1 lime juiced
- ¼ tsp paprika
- ¼ tsp cumin powder
- 2 tbsp parsley chopped
- 2 tbsp cilantro chopped
- 1 green chili chopped -seed out or in depending on the heat level

Method

1. Pour 1 cup of water into the inner pot
2. Insert steamer rack and place the salmon fillets
3. Pressure cook for 5 minutes. Release pressure quickly
4. While salmon is being cooked, combine all the sauce ingredients, and make a smooth paste in a food processor.
5. Pour over hot salmon and let it sit for 1 minute

SPICY BAKED CATFISH IN BANANA LEAF

Ingredients

- 2 4 oz catfish filets
- 1 tsp olive oil or butter
- Salt to taste
- 1 sliced tomato
- ¼ tsp paprika
- ½ tsp curry powder
- 2 springs curry leaves
- 1 green chili chopped -seed out or in depending on the heat level

Method

1. In a banana leaf season both sides of the catfish fillets with spices, salt, and olive oil. Place tomato and onion slices, jalapenos and curry leaves (1 spring for each fillet)
2. Wrap the banana leaf around the fillet. Tie it with baking or cooking twine.
3. Insert steamer rack and place the banana leaf-wrapped fish
4. Pressure cook for 5 minutes. Release pressure quickly

Recipe Note:

1. If the banana leaf is not available, any other edible leaves such as cabbage leaves, collard green leaves, grape leaves may be used. Aluminum foil may be used as wrap as well.

SHRIMP WITH ASPARAGUS

Basic Ingredients

- 1 lb peeled and deveined shrimp
- ½ lb asparagus washed and cut into 2 inch pieces
- 2 tsp butter
- ½ cup cilantro
- ½ turmeric powder
- ¼ tsp pepper powder
- 1 lemon juiced
- Salt to taste

Method

1. Set the instant pot to sauté. Add butter, once melted, add turmeric and pepper powder. Sauté for 1 minute.
2. Add Asparagus and shrimp, mix well.
3. Close the lid and set the valve in the sealing position.
4. Cook on low pressure for 5 minutes manual setting
5. Release pressure immediately
6. Add lime juice and cilantro.

CHAPTER 5. COOKING MEAT DISHES

Meats need more time to cook than grains, vegetables, and seafood. Typically, beef requires about 20-25 minutes per 1 pound of meat while lamb, goat, and pork require about 15 minutes, and chicken about 8 minutes per pound. Meat cooked in larger pieces or full chicken may take additional time. The cooking time also needs to be adjusted based on the cut of meat as I do when I buy cheaper meat and make it a nice dish by cooking well and adding spices and herbs. In such cases, add about 5 more minutes to cooking time.

BEEF AND CASSAVA

Ingredients

- 2 lb. beef cut into small pieces (with bone or without)
- 2 lb. cassava peeled, washed and cut into 1-inch pieces (frozen sliced cassava may be used as well)
- 2 tsp coconut oil (olive oil or vegetable oil can be used as well)
- 1/2 tsp turmeric powder
- 1-2 tsp black pepper powder
- 2 tsp coriander powder
- 2 large onion sliced
- 2-inch piece of ginger thinly sliced
- ½ - 1 tsp salt or to taste
- 2-3 medium tomato sliced
- 4-6 cloves of garlic crushed
- Cilantro – 1 cup (optional)
- ½ - 1 cup water/beef stock/bone broth

Method

1. Sprinkle ½ teaspoon of turmeric powder, 1 tsp coriander powder, ½ tsp cumin powder and salt on the washed and cut beef pieces, mix well, and set aside for 20 minutes.
2. Set instant pot to sauté and add oil. Add onions, garlic, and ginger. Stir until golden.
3. Add coriander powder, pepper powder, and turmeric. Stir for 2-3 minutes.
4. Add tomato and mix well.
5. Add beef and cassava. Add salt. Mix well. Add sufficient water/broth (usually ¾ of a cup) so that there is enough water to build steam in the cooker.
6. Close the lid and set it to meat and cook until done.
7. Release steam naturally. Garnish with cilantro and serve

Recipe Notes:

1. In most cases, water and juices from beef and cassava are enough to pressure cook the dish. But while mixing and transferring the contents to the cooker, ½ cup - 1 cup water or beef broth may be added to make sure there is enough water for pressure cooking.
2. The spices may be sautéed in an instant pot set to sauté mode or in a pressure cooker on an open stove. In that case, there is no need to transfer the contents from sautéing pan to the pressure cooker.
3. Instead of the pressure cooker, a crockpot or a stovetop utensil may be used. In this case, cover the

pot and cook on low-medium heat until the beef is well cooked.

4. Alternatively, cassava and beef may be cooked separately and mixed with spices. In this case, follow the steps below
   a. Cook marinated beef and set aside
   b. Cook cassava with salt (boil with sufficient water, drain) and set aside
   c. Follow steps 2,3 and 4 to make a cooked masala
   d. Add cooked beef, cassava and mix well. Add cilantro, additional salt if needed and serve.

BEEF/CHICKEN PEPPER FRY

Ingredients

- 2 lb boneless chicken breast/beef cut into 1 inch cubes/strips
- 2 tsp coconut oil (olive oil or vegetable oil can be used as well)
- 1/2 tsp turmeric powder
- 1-2 tsp black pepper powder
- 2 tsp coriander powder
- 2 large onion sliced
- 2 inch piece of ginger thinly sliced
- Salt
- 2-3 medium tomato sliced
- 4-6 cloves of garlic crushed
- Cilantro – 1 cup (optional)

Method

1. Set instant pot to saute and add oil. Add onions, garlic, and ginger. Stir until golden.
2. Add coriander powder, pepper powder, and turmeric. Stir for 2-3 minutes.
3. Add tomato and mix well.
4. Add chicken and mix so that chicken is coated well with spices and onion.
5. Close the lid and pressure cook for about 8 minutes. Water in tomato and chicken should be sufficient to pressure cook.
6. Once done, release the steam instantly.
7. Switch the instant pot back to saute again and mix well until some of the water evaporates.
8. Garnish with cilantro. Serve with rice or naan (Indian bread).

KALE AND CHICKEN FRY

This is something I tried recently and found good. The simplest way to make this is to make chicken with spices following any one of the recipes above, make kale chips and just crumble the chips into the chicken and mix well.

Ingredients

- 2 lb boneless chicken breast/beef cut into 1 inch cubes/strips
- 2 tsp coconut oil (olive oil or vegetable oil can be used as well)
- 1/2 tsp turmeric powder
- 1-2 tsp black pepper powder
- 2 tsp coriander powder

- 2 large onion sliced
- 2 inch piece of ginger thinly sliced
- Salt to taste
- 2-3 medium tomato sliced
- 4-6 cloves of garlic crushed
- Cilantro – 1 cup (optional)
- 2 cups of green or red kale washed and cut/tore into 1-2 inch pieces (to make kale chips)

Method

1. Set instant pot to sauté setting; add coconut oil, onions, garlic and ginger. Stir until golden.
2. Add coriander powder, pepper powder and turmeric, stir for one minute and then add tomato and mix well.
3. Add chicken mix so that chicken is coated well with spices and onion.
4. Cover the instant pot. Set to poultry and cook.
5. Meanwhile in parallel, spread the kale pieces on a cookie sheet and put in the oven at 350 degrees for 10 minutes or the kale become chips and can easily crumble.
6. Once the instant pot cooking is done. Release the pressure immediately, take the kale chips and crumble using your hand and spread it on top of chicken fry.
7. Mix well and cover it for 1 minute. Garnish with cilantro. Serve with rice or naan (Indian bread).

BELL PEPPER AND CHICKEN STIR FRY

Basic Ingredients

- 1 bell pepper washed and cut into thin slices (use the different color peppers as you desire)
- 2 tsp coconut oil (olive oil or vegetable oil can be used as well)
- 1 lb boneless chicken breast cut into thin strips
- 1 tsp turmeric powder
- 1 tsp black pepper powder
- 1 tsp coriander powder
- 1 medium onion sliced
- ½ inch piece of ginger thinly sliced
- Salt to taste
- 1-2 medium tomato sliced
- 3 cloves of garlic crushed

Optional Ingredients

- 1 Jalapeño pepper sliced into thin pieces
- ¼ cup cilantro chopped

Method

1. Sprinkle ½ spoons of turmeric powder, pepper powder, and salt on the washed and cut chicken, mix well, and set aside for 10 minutes.
2. In a pan, heat oil, add onions, crushed garlic, ginger, and optional Jalapeno. Sauté till onions become translucent.
3. Add rest of turmeric powder, coriander powder, and pepper powder and mix well.
4. Add tomato and mix.

5. Now add the bell pepper and chicken and mix well.
6. Cover and cook for 10 minutes on medium heat or until chicken and peppers are cooked. Stir occasionally.
7. Switch off the heat, add optional cilantro, add more salt if required depending on your taste.

Serve with rice or bread

SPICY BEEF AND POTATO STU

Basic Ingredients

- 1-1/2 lb beef cut into ½ inch cubes
- 3 medium potatoes, washed, peeled and cut into 1 inch cubes
- 2 tbsp – coriander powder
- 1 tbsp – cumin powder
- 1 tsp – turmeric powder
- ½ tsp – black pepper powder
- 2 green chilies slit (optional)
- 2 tsp ginger garlic paste (or 1 tsp grated ginger and 3-4 garlic crushed garlic cloves)
- 1 cup coriander leaves
- 1 onion chopped
- 2 medium tomatoes chopped
- Salt to taste
-

Method

1. Sprinkle ½ teaspoon of turmeric powder, 1 tsp coriander powder, ½ tsp cumin powder and salt on

the washed and cut beef pieces, mix well, and set aside for 20 minutes.

2. Instant pot set to sauté, heat oil, add onions, crushed garlic, ginger, and optional Jalapeno. Sauté till onions become translucent.
3. Add rest of turmeric powder, coriander powder, cumin powder, and pepper powder and mix well.
4. Add tomato and mix.
5. Now add beef pieces
6. Set one pot to meat. Cover and cook. After cooking, release the steam naturally
7. Add optional cilantro, add more salt if required depending on your taste.

Serve with rice or bread

SPICY GOAT CURRY

Basic Ingredients

- 2 lbs. bone-in goat pieces
- 2 tsp – coriander powder
- 1 tsp – cumin powder
- 1 tsp – turmeric powder
- ½ tsp – black pepper powder
- 1 tsp garam masala
- 1 tsp paprika
- 3-4 whole cloves
- 2-3 green cardamom
- 2 green chilies slit (optional)
- 2 tsp ginger garlic paste (or 1 tsp grated ginger and 3-4 garlic crushed garlic cloves)
- 2 bay leaves
- 1 onion chopped
- 2 medium tomatoes chopped
- Salt to taste
-

Method

1. Sprinkle ½ teaspoon of turmeric powder, 1 tsp coriander powder, ½ tsp cumin powder and salt on the goat pieces. Mix well and set aside for 20 minutes.
2. Instant pot set to saute, heat oil, add onions, crushed garlic, ginger, and optional Jalapeno. Sauté till onions become translucent.

3. Add rest of turmeric powder, coriander powder, cumin powder, and other spices and sauté for about 1-2 minutes.
4. Add tomato and mix.
5. Now add goat pieces and mix well for about 1 minute so the marinade on the goat pieces gets cooked.
6. Set one pot to meat. Cover and cook. If you are using manual cooking, set high pressure, and cook for about 40 minutes. After cooking, release the steam naturally
7. Open lid. Add optional cilantro, add more salt if required depending on your taste.

Recipe Notes:

Instead of goat, lamb meat may be prepared using the same recipe.

COCONUT CURRY CHICKEN

Basic Ingredients

- 1-1/2 pound chicken breast cut into small (1 inch) pieces
- 2-4 spoons of curry powder depending on your tolerance on spice
- 1 tsp turmeric
- 1` medium onion chopped
- 2-3 tsp oil
- ½ tsp pepper powder
- 2 medium potatoes – peeled and cut into 1 inch cubes
- 3-4 cloves of garlic crushed
- ½ inch cube of ginger peeled and sliced

- 1 can (14 oz) of coconut milk
- ¼ cup mint leaves or cilantro
- Salt to taste
- ½ -1 can of chicken broth (depending on the amount gravy desired)

Optional Ingredients

- 1 cup carrot sliced
- 2 medium chopped tomatoes

Method

1. Sprinkle 1 tsp curry powder, ½ turmeric, and ¼ tsp salt on cut chicken. Mix well and keep it aside for 10 minutes.
2. In a separate pan, heat oil, sauté onions, garlic, and ginger until onions become translucent.
3. Add remaining curry powder, turmeric and pepper powder. Mix for 1-2 minutes.
4. Add chicken, potato, and optional tomato and carrot. Mix well 1-2 minutes until the chicken and potato are coated with the gravy.
5. Add chicken broth and coconut milk and close the lid
6. Cook in manual setting for 15 minutes.
7. Once cooked, release the steam naturally
8. Open lid and add mint leaves/cilantro and stir. Add salt to taste.

Serve with rice or bread.

BEEF AND VEGETABLE STEW

Basic Ingredients

- 1-1/2 pound beef cut into ½ inch pieces
- 2-4 spoons of curry powder depending on your tolerance on spice
- 1 tsp turmeric
- 2 medium onion chopped
- 2-3 tsp coconut oil
- ½ tsp pepper powder
- 2 medium potatoes – peeled and cut into 1 inch cubes
- 1 cup carrots chopped
- 1 cup cut celery stocks
- 3-4 cloves of garlic crushed
- ½ inch cube of ginger peeled and sliced
- ¼ cup mint leaves or cilantro
- Salt to taste
- 2-3 cups of beef or vegetable broth (depending on the amount gravy desired)

Method

1. Sprinkle 1 tsp curry powder, ½ turmeric, and ¼ tsp salt on cut beef. Mix well and keep it aside for 10 minutes.
2. In a separate pan, heat oil, sauté onions, garlic, and ginger until onions become translucent.
3. Add remaining curry powder, turmeric, and pepper powder. Mix for 1-2 minutes.

4. Add beef, potato, celery, carrots, and tomato. Mix well 1-2 minutes until the beef and vegetable are coated with the gravy.
5. Add broth and close the lid
6. Cook in manual setting for 25 minutes.
7. Once cooked, release the steam naturally
8. Open the lid and add mint leaves/cilantro and stir. Add salt to taste.

Serve with rice or bread.

CHAPTER 6. COOKING VEGETARIAN

Most vegetables take less than 5 minutes to cook in the instant pot. Carrots, whole potatoes, sweet potatoes or yams may take anywhere from 8-10 minutes. Keep this in mind while cooking a mix of these vegetables.

CAULIFLOWER AND POTATO

Basic Ingredients

- 2 medium potatoes, peeled and cut into 1 inch cubes
- ½ head of cauliflower washed and cut into pieces (same size as potato)
- 2 tsp oil
- ½ tsp black pepper powder
- 1 medium onion sliced
- 1 tsp turmeric
- 1-2 medium tomato chopped
- Salt to taste
- ¼ cup cilantro chopped
- Vegetable broth – 1/2 cup

Optional Ingredients
- ½ tsp cumin seeds
- 1-2 jalapenos sliced (seed out/in)
- 2-3 cloves of garlic crushed
- ½ inch ginger chopped into fine pieces
- ½-1 tsp curry powder
- 1 tsp lemon juice

Method

1. Set instant pot to sauté. Add oil and crackle optional cumin seeds
2. Add onions, optional garlic, ginger, and jalapenos; sauté until onions are golden brown.
3. Add turmeric, pepper, and optional curry powder and stir for 1-2 minutes.
4. Add chopped tomatoes, potatoes and cook for about 5 minutes.
5. Add cauliflower, mix well and then add vegetable broth
6. Close the lid and set instant pot to vegetable setting and cook. In manual mode set high pressure, about 4 minutes.
7. Release pressure by quick release. Add cilantro, salt, and optional lemon juice.

Mix well and serve hot as a side dish with rice or bread.

Note 1: There are many optional ingredients listed, one could use all of them or pick and choose based on your taste.

Note 2: The jalapenos vary in their heat level. If you choose to use them, you can take seeds out to reduce the heat. This note applies to all the recipes in this book.

VEGETABLE STIR-FRY

Basic Ingredients

- 4 cups chopped up mixed vegetables – carrots, broccoli, cauliflower, beans and bell pepper
- 2 tsp coconut or olive oil
- ½ tsp black pepper powder
- 1 medium onion sliced
- 1 tsp turmeric
- 1-2 medium tomato chopped
- Salt to taste
- ¼ cup cilantro chopped
- Vegetable broth – 1/2 cup

Optional Ingredients
- ½ tsp cumin seeds
- 1-2 jalapenos sliced (seed out/in)
- 2-3 cloves of garlic crushed
- ½ inch ginger chopped into fine pieces
- ½-1 tsp curry powder
- 1 tsp lemon juice

Method

1. Set instant pot to sauté. Add oil and crackle optional cumin seeds
2. Add onions, optional garlic, ginger, and jalapenos; sauté until onions are golden brown.
3. Add turmeric, pepper, and optional curry powder and stir for 1-2 minutes.
4. Add chopped tomatoes, cook for about 5 minutes.
5. Add chopped up vegetable mix well for about 2 minutes.

6. Close the lid and set instant pot to vegetable setting and cook. In manual mode set high pressure, about 2 minutes.
7. Release pressure by a quick release. Add cilantro, salt and optional lemon juice.

Mix well and serve hot as a side dish with rice or bread.

Recipe Notes:

1. There are many optional ingredients listed, one could use all of them or pick and choose based on your taste.
2. The jalapenos vary in their heat level. If you choose to use them, you can take seeds out to reduce the heat. This note applies to all the recipes in this book.
3. The ingredients list has ½ cup broth. However, the water from vegetables and tomatoes will be sufficient to cook this dish. Adding broth may result in a curry instead of stir fry.

BROCCOLI STIR-FRY

Ingredients

- 4 cups broccoli florets
- 2 tsp coconut or olive oil
- ½ tsp black pepper powder
- 1 medium onion sliced
- 1 tsp turmeric
- Salt to taste
- ¼ cup cilantro chopped
- Vegetable broth – 1/2 cup
- ½ tsp cumin seeds
- ½ tsp mustard seeds
- 1-2 jalapenos sliced (seed out/in)
- 2-3 cloves of garlic crushed
- 1 tsp lemon juice

Method

1. Set instant pot to sauté. Add oil and crackle mustard and cumin seeds
2. Add onions, garlic, and jalapenos; sauté until onions are golden brown.
3. Add turmeric, pepper and stir for 1-2 minutes.
4. Add broccoli florets and mix well for about 2 minutes. Add ¼ cup vegetable broth or just enough to build steam in the cooker
5. Close the lid and set instant pot to vegetable setting and cook. In manual mode set high pressure, about 2 minutes.
6. Release pressure by quick release. Add cilantro, salt, and lemon juice. Mix well and serve hot as a side dish with rice or bread.

EGGPLANT CURRY

Ingredients

- 1 large eggplant coconut oil
- 3 cloves of garlic chopped
- 1 cup finely chopped onions
- 1 cup finely chopped tomatoes
- ¼ tsp chili powder (use mild, medium or hot depending on your heat tolerance level)
- ½ tsp garam masala
- ¼ cup cilantro
- 2 tsp lime juice (optional)
- Salt to taste

Method

1. Flame or oven roast the eggplant. In the oven, use the broil setting to get the eggplant cooked and the skin charred. Make sure to turn the eggplant over so the cooking is even all around. If you are using an open flame, use the same guideline to cook it evenly and get the skin charred so it can be peeled off easily.
2. Let the eggplant cool down. Peel the skin away and mash the remaining eggplant into a fine lump.
3. Instant pot set to saute, add oil and sauté onions until golden brown. Add chili powder and garam masala and mix well. Add tomatoes and mashed eggplant and mix well.
4. Close the lid and pressure cook in manual mode for 10 minutes.
5. Release steam naturally, Open the lid and add cilantro and lime juice, mix well and serve hot.

INSTANT POT LENTIL RECIPES

Legumes and lentils are some of the healthiest foods by virtue of their low fat and low sugar. They are also high in fiber and protein. Lentils are even more important as a source of protein as part of a vegan diet. Some lentil variety, such as black beans, has anti-cancer properties. Lentils are also beneficial as part of a diet that helps with weight loss, heart-healthy, cholesterol-busting food regime.

Cooking lentils in an instant pot is pretty easy. Lentils being dried grains, it takes more time to cook than regular vegetables. The easiest way to cook lentils to soak them in water prior to cooking them. An instant pot electric pressure cooker or manual cooker can cut cooking down into half and also cook them much better than the regular stovetop cooking. Typically, dried lentils take anywhere between 20 and 40 minutes to cook depending on the type of lentils. Soaked lentils can cut down the cooking time by more than half.

There are literally hundreds of recipes for making lentil-based curry depending on the type of lentil used, spices and herbs used, and any other vegetables are added in making the curry.

Whole lentil or split lentil may be used for making lentil curry. Typically, lentil curry is prepared with lentils as the only ingredient other than spices and herbs sautéed with onions. The following vegetables may be added while cooking lentils to make different lentil preparations:

- Tomato

- Potato
- Celery
- Carrot
- Spinach
- Cabbage
- Bell pepper
- Eggplant
- Snake gourd
- Okra
- Broccoli
- Cauliflower
- Butternut squash
- Pumpkin
- Beans
- Peas
- A mix of other legumes
- Various types of gourds

The simplest way to add these veggies to lentil is to cook them together in a pressure cooker. The vegetables will get cooked very well along with lentils and will enhance the overall nutrition and flavor. You can add one or more of these vegetables but keep the proportion to 1 cup lentil to 2 cups or less of vegetables to keep the lentil curry more balanced.

Curry powder blend or paste of your choice or individual spices may be used in the preparation of lentil curry. The same preparation may be used for other legumes such as chickpeas, peas, kidney beans, and more.

By using different spice blends, one can create different versions of lentil curry. In its simplest form, cooked lentil is mixed with onions sautéed in coconut or vegetable oil with a teaspoon of turmeric.

Below are several recipes.

LENTIL CURRY RECIPE #1 (SIMPLE VERSION)

Ingredients

- 2 cups of red lentils (split or whole) washed
- 1 tsp turmeric powder
- ¼ black pepper powder
- 4 garlic cloves chopped
- 1 tsp grated ginger
- 2 medium onions chopped
- 2 tsp lemon juice
- 2 tsp coconut or vegetable oil
- ½ cup cilantro, chopped
- Salt to taste
- 5-6 cups of water

Method

1. Set the instant pot to sauté mode add oil. Add onions, garlic, and ginger and sauté until onions become translucent. Add turmeric and pepper powder. Mix well a couple of minutes until the spices get cooked.
2. Add the lentil and water. Close the lid. Set the instant pot to beans.
3. Once cooked, let the pressure of naturally. Open the lid. Add salt, cilantro, and lemon juice. Mix well.

Serve with Jasmin rice.

LENTIL CURRY RECIPE #2

Ingredients

- 2 cups of red lentils (split or whole)
- 1-2 tsp curry powder (mild, medium or hot depending on your tolerance level)
- 1 tsp cumin
- 1 tsp turmeric powder
- 1 jalapeño split lengthwise
- 4 garlic cloves chopped
- 1 tsp ginger grated
- 2 medium onions chopped
- 3 medium tomatoes sliced
- 2 cups of celery chopped
- 2 tsp coconut or vegetable oil
- ½ cup cilantro, chopped
- Salt to taste
- 5-6 cups of water/broth

Method

1. Set the instant pot to sauté. Add oil and crackle cumin. Add onions, jalapenos, garlic, and ginger. Sauté until onions become translucent. Add turmeric and curry powder. Mix well until the spices are cooked.
2. Add the lentil, tomatoes, and celery. Mix well for 1-2 minutes. Add water. Close the lid. Set the instant pot to beans and cook.
3. Release steam naturally. Open the lid. Add salt and cilantro. Mix well. Serve with Jasmin rice.

LENTIL AND SPINACH CURRY

Ingredients

- 1 cups of red lentils (split or whole)
- 1 bunches of spinach washed and chopped
- 1-2 tsp curry powder (optional)
- 1 tsp cumin
- 1 tsp turmeric powder
- ¼ black pepper powder
- 1 jalapeño split lengthwise
- 2 medium onions chopped
- 3 medium tomatoes sliced
- 2 tsp coconut or vegetable oil
- ½ cup cilantro, chopped
- Salt to taste
- 5-6 cups of water/broth

Method

1. Set the instant pot to sauté mode add oil. Crackle cumin. Add onions, jalapenos and sauté until onions become translucent. Add turmeric and curry powder. Mix well until the spices are cooked.
2. Add the lentil, tomatoes. Mix well for 1-2 minutes. Add spinach and water. Close the lid. Set the instant pot to beans and cook.
3. Once cooked, let the pressure of naturally. Open the lid. Add salt and cilantro. Mix well.

Serve with Jasmin rice.

QUICK AND EASY CHICKPEAS CURRY

Ingredients

- 1 cup chickpeas soaked in water overnight
- 1 cup curry paste
- 1 tsp cumin
- 2 medium onions chopped
- 2 tsp coconut or vegetable oil
- ½ cup cilantro, chopped
- Salt to taste
- 3 cups of water

Method

1. Cook the chickpeas in a pressure cooker with 3-4 cups of water and set aside.
2. Heat oil in a pan. Crackle cumin. Add onions and sauté until onions become translucent.
3. Add curry paste. Mix it well. Add cilantro.
4. Now add the chickpeas and bring to boil.

QUICK AND EASY CANNED GARBANZO BEANS CURRY

Ingredients

- 2 cans of garbanzo beans
- 1 cup curry paste
- ½ cup cilantro, chopped
- Salt to taste

Method

1. In a pan mix the garbanzo beans with curry paste.
2. Bring it to a boil. Add ½ cup water if needed.
3. Add cilantro. Cover and simmer for 5 minutes.

CHAPTER 7. BROTHS

Broth recipes are very easy to make in an instant pot due to its automatic and timer features. Most vegetable broths can be cooked in 30-40 minutes under high-pressure setting. Bone broth typically takes several hours to cook in traditional cooking, but instant pot cuts down the cooking time of bone broth in half or even less.

Typically, broths are not considered a mainstream Indian dish. However, in parts of India, such as south where my parents lived, my mom used to make bone soup for my dad using traditional utensils. She cooked overnight and used ginger, garlic, turmeric, and other spices liberally.

VEGAN BROTH

This is a simple broth that provides healing at and helps with minor ailments such as cold and flu. This is fully vegan and contains nutrients from a number of vegetables and herbs.

Ingredients

- 2-3 celery sticks cut into inch pieces
- 3 medium tomatoes chopped
- 1 bell pepper cut into pieces
- 1 large onion peeled and cut into pieces
- 1 pound (2-3 medium) carrots washed cut into pieces
- 1 cup kale
- 1 medium beetroot washed and cut into pieces
- ½ cup parsley chopped
- ½ cup cilantro chopped
- 3-4 garlic cloves crushed

- 3-4 whole cloves
- 5-6 black peppercorns or ½ tsp pepper powder
- 1-2 bay leaves
- 1 gallon water
- Salt to taste (if you must or avoid salt)

Method

1. Add everything to the instant pot.

2. Set it to manual and select high pressure and 40 minutes of cooking time.

3. Allow natural steam release. Open the lid and strain the broth into a large bowl

4. Add salt to taste, add some chopped fresh herbs of your choice and serve warm.

5. Refrigerate any remaining broth

6. The strained vegetables are pretty good and can be eaten separately or pureed in a blender used.

SPICY VEGAN BROTH

This is a spicy version of the vegan broth that immediately helps with congestion, cold, flu, sore throat and other ailments due to infections. Like the non-spicy version, this broth also is healing and easy for your gut. The anti-oxidants and anti-inflammatory compounds in turmeric and ginger make this broth even healthier.

Ingredients: Veggies

- 2-3 celery sticks cut into inch pieces

- 3 medium tomatoes chopped
- 1 bell green pepper cut into pieces
- 1 red bell pepper cut into pieces
- ¼ of a medium red cabbage chopped
- 1 large onion peeled and cut into 1 inch cubes
- ½ cup chopped onion (for sautéing)
- 1 pound (2-3 medium) carrots washed cut into pieces
- 1 cup kale
- 1 medium beetroot washed and cut into pieces

Ingredients – spices and herbs
- ½ cup parsley chopped
- ½ cup cilantro chopped
- 3-4 garlic cloves crushed
- 3-4 whole cloves
- 5-6 black peppercorns or ½ tsp pepper powder
- 1-2 bay leaves
- 1 inch ginger finely chopped
- 2 tsp turmeric powder or 2 inch fresh root
- 2 jalapeño pepper sliced lengthwise (seed in or out depending on your heat tolerance)
- ½ tsp cayenne powder
- ½ tsp cumin powder
- 1 gallon water
- Salt to taste (if you must or avoid salt)
- 1 tsp coconut or vegetable oil

Method

1. Instant pot set to saute, heat oil and add onions, crushed garlic, ginger, jalapeño peppers.

2. Sauté for 2-3 minutes or until onions become translucent. Add all the spices (cayenne, cumin,

turmeric, cloves, bay leaves pepper powder) and sauté for another 2-3 minutes so the spices are blended well (make sure not to burn the spices).

4. Add all the vegetables into the instant pot and add water and close the lid.

5. Set it to manual and select high pressure and 40 minutes of cooking time.

6. Allow natural steam release. Open the lid and strain the broth into a large bowl

7. Add salt to taste, add some chopped fresh herbs of your choice and serve warm.

8. Refrigerate any remaining broth

The strained-out vegetables are also nutritious and may be consumed separately.

BONE BROTHS

Instant Pot cuts down cooking time for bone broth significantly as the contents are cooked under high pressure. Instead of 12 hrs – 24hrs simmering, bone broth can be made easily using an instant pot in about one hour. While recipes using instant pot calls for 1 hour of cooking, one can certainly increase the cooking time to several hours or overnight. The more bones are cooked, the better in extracting the nutrients from them.

Bone broth is considered a new age miracle drink. It is gaining popularity with athletes and celebrities as a wellness drink. By combining the immense benefits of nutrients and minerals in traditional bone broth with the medicinal properties of spices and herbs, we can make an even more potent and healthful drink. Below are some of the benefits of these spicy bone broths:

Antioxidant: Contents in bone broth such as glycine and gelatin both contain antioxidants which, coupled with antioxidants in spices such as turmeric and ginger, make bone broth one of the best sources of antioxidants. As noted in my other books, antioxidants fight free radicals (which cause cancer and other debilitating diseases).

Anti-inflammatory: By adding ginger, garlic, chili powder, and turmeric in the preparation of bone broth, one enhances the anti-inflammatory properties of the broth.

Detoxification: Bone broth made by adding vegetables that contain sulfur helps the body to manufacture detox agents such as glutathione (amino acid). These detox agents help your kidneys to detox heavy metals from the body.

Bone health: Bone broth is an excellent source of calcium, magnesium and phosphorous, which help bones to stay strong and healthy.

Fight infections: As a result of enhanced immunity and a strong digestive system, bone broth helps fight infections.

Improves immunity: Minerals and amino acids in bone broth help improve the immune system.

Speedy recovery: With so many benefits such as boosting the immune system, improving the digestive system, and fighting infection, it is no wonder bone broth helps in speedy recovery of the body from common ailments. Spicy bone broth could aid in recovering from conditions such as cold & flu, nausea, and diarrhea.

Gut cleaning: Bone broth helps proper digestion of food and keeps your gut and digestive system healthy.

Improves joints: Bone broth contains glucosamine and chondroitin, which help to maintain joints and keep them healthy and strong.

Helps athletic performance: Healthy joints and bones help improve your athleticism and reduce joint pain after exercise.

Improves metabolism and helps weight loss: An improved digestive system and a healthy gut help promote proper metabolism and weight loss.

Beauty enhancer: Collagen in bone broth helps skin, hair, and nails to be healthy and shiny.

Weight Loss: Any time your weight is more than 20% of your normal range, one should seriously consider ways to reduce weight. Obesity is one of the most significant causes of many health problems. Bone broth diet is light in calories and high in nutrients and can be incorporated as part of a weight-loss diet plan.

As you see from the above benefits, when combined with healthful vegetables and medicinal spices and herbs, bone broth indeed becomes a miracle drink that improves your health, boosts immunity, fights diseases, and keeps you feeling young. By adding spices and herbs to the bone broth, additional benefits below are accrued. These additional benefits are due to the antioxidant, anti-cancer, anti-inflammatory, and other benefits of the spice and herb ingredients.

Bone Broth Recipes

The main ingredient in bone broth is some type of bone, one can mix and match additional ingredients depending on your taste, the kind of flavor you like, and the level of spiciness you can tolerate. Usually, one or more of the following bones are used as part of the bone broth:

- Chicken
- Turkey
- Fish
- Beef
- Lamb or Goat
- Pork

One has a large choice of vegetables.

- Carrots
- Celery
- Tomatoes
- Bell pepper – all colors

- Beetroot

- Onions

- Kale

- Red cabbage

Spices and herbs: One or more of the following spices and herbs may be used.

- Turmeric (powder or root)

- Ginger root

- Garlic

- Bay leaves

- Whole cloves

- Black peppers

- Curry powder

- Parsley

- Cilantro

- Thyme

- Rosemary

- Oregano

- Cumin seeds or cumin powder

- Fennel seeds or fennel powder

- Cinnamon

Others:

Apple Cider Vinegar

EASY BONE BROTH (CHICKEN)

This is one of the easiest ways to make bone broth. I make it out of the carcass from the rotisserie chicken bought from the departmental store. I remove all the meat and use it as a regular meal for the family and use the entire carcass (without the skins – but skins may be used as well if you prefer) for the bone broth

Ingredients

- Chicken carcass from a full rotisserie chicken – skin and fat optional
- 4 celery sticks cut into 1 inch pieces
- 3 medium tomatoes chopped
- 1 bell pepper cut into pieces (any color)
- 1 large onion peeled and quartered
- 1 pound (2-3 medium) carrots washed cut into pieces
- ½ cup parsley chopped
- ½ cup cilantro chopped
- 3-4 garlic cloves crushed
- 3-4 whole cloves
- 2 inch ginger peeled and grated
- 5-6 black peppercorns or ½ tsp pepper powder
- 1-2 bay leaves
- 1 Jalapeño pepper slit (optional)
- 1 gallon water
- Salt to taste (if you must or avoid salt)

Method

1. Add all the ingredients into the instant pot. Add enough water to cover all the vegetables and bones. Add vinegar.

2. Close the lid. Set the instant pot on manual setting – high pressure and 60 minutes timer.

3. Once the bones and vegetables are cooked, strain the broth into a large bowl

4. Add salt to taste, add some chopped fresh herbs of your choice and serve warm.

5. Refrigerate any remaining broth

Recipe Notes:

1. The strained vegetables are pretty good and can be eaten after removing all the bone pieces.

2. A slow cooker or a manual pressure cooker may be used for cooking.

3. You can make this broth a meal by making it a soup. For making it a soup – add ½ cup split lentils, ½ cup brown or white rice to the pot. Use a large mesh strainer to strain so the cooked rice and lentils pass through. Add some of the vegetables back and enjoy it especially when you are recovering from illness or when you don't feel like having a full meal but something filling and nutritious.

SPICY BONE BROTH (CHICKEN-SPICY)

This is a spicy version of the previous chicken bone broth. This spicy broth immediately helps with congestion, cold, flu, sore throat, and other ailments due to infections. This broth also is healing and easy for your gut besides all the long-term health benefits that come with regular consumption of these bone broth and healing spices.

Basic Ingredients:

- 4 lb chicken bones – any combination of wings, necks and feet.
- 4 celery sticks cut into 1 inch pieces
- 3 medium tomatoes chopped
- 1 bell pepper cut into pieces (any color)
- 1 large onion peeled and quartered
- 1 pound (2-3 medium) carrots washed cut into pieces
- 1 gallon of water
- 2 tablespoon raw unfiltered apple cider vinegar
- Salt to taste (if you must or avoid salt)

Spices & Herbs

- 2 tsp turmeric powder
- 1 tsp cumin powder or 1tsp cumin seeds
- 1 tsp coriander powder
- 1 tsp cayenne powder
- 2 tsp fenugreek seeds
- ½ cup parsley chopped
- ½ cup cilantro chopped
- ½ cup rosemary

- 3-4 garlic cloves crushed
- 3-4 whole cloves
- 2 inch ginger peeled and grated
- 5-6 black peppercorns or ½ tsp pepper powder
- 1-2 bay leaves
- 1-2 Jalapeño pepper slit (optional)

Method

1. The instant pot is set to sauté function, heat 2 tbsp olive oil, crackle cumin seeds and fenugreek seeds. Add onions, crushed garlic, ginger, jalapeño peppers

2. Sauté for 2-3 minutes or until onions becomes translucent. Add all the spices (cayenne, cumin, turmeric, coriander, cloves, bay leaves, and pepper powder) and sauté for another 2-3 minutes so the spices are blended well and sufficiently roasted (make sure not to burn the spices).

3. Add all chicken bones and vegetables. Add enough water to cover all the vegetables and bones. Add vinegar.

4. Close the lid. Set the instant pot on manual setting – low pressure and 12-hour timer.

5. Once the bones and vegetables are cooked, strain the broth into a large bowl

6. Add salt to taste, add some chopped fresh herbs of your choice, and serve warm.

7. Refrigerate any remaining broth

BONE BROTH (BEEF)

Ingredients:

- 4 lb beef bones – a mix of marrow bones, knuckle bones, short ribs
- 4 celery sticks cut into 1 inch pieces
- 3 medium tomatoes chopped
- 1 large onion peeled and quartered
- 1 pound (2-3 medium) carrots washed cut into pieces
- 3-4 beets with leaves. Leaves chopped. Beets peeled and cut into pieces
- 2 inch ginger piece peeled and grated
- 3-4 cloves of garlic
- 1 gallon of water
- Salt to taste
- Pepper to taste
- ½ cup cilantro
- ½ cup parsley
- 2 tablespoon apple cider vinegar

Method

1. Add all beef bones, vegetables, spices and herbs into the instant pot. Add enough water to cover all the vegetables and bones. Add vinegar.

2. Close the lid. Set the instant pot on manual setting – low pressure and 24 hour timer.

3. Once the bones and vegetables are cooked, strain the broth into a large bowl

4. Add salt to taste, add some chopped fresh herbs of your choice, and serve warm.

5. Refrigerate any remaining broth

BEEF BONE BROTH (ROASTED - SPICY)

This is a spicy version of the previous beef bone broth.

Basic Ingredients:

- 4 lb beef bones – a mix of marrow bones, knuckle bones, short ribs
- 4 celery stalks cut into 1 inch pieces
- 3 medium tomatoes chopped
- 1 bell pepper cut into pieces (any color)
- 1 large onion peeled and quartered
- 1 pound (2-3 medium) carrots washed cut into pieces
- 1 gallon water
- 3 tablespoon raw unfiltered apple cider vinegar
- Salt to taste (if you must or avoid salt)
- 2 tsp coconut oil

Spices & Herbs

- 2 tsp turmeric powder
- 1 tsp cumin powder or 1tsp cumin seeds
- 1 tsp coriander powder
- 1 tsp cayenne powder
- 2 tsp fenugreek seeds
- ½ cup parsley chopped
- ½ cup cilantro chopped

- ½ cup rosemary
- 3-4 garlic cloves crushed
- 3-4 whole cloves
- 2 inch ginger peeled and grated
- 5-6 black peppercorns or ½ tsp pepper powder
- 1-2 bay leaves
- 1-2 Jalapeño pepper slit (optional)

Method

1. Set oven to 350 degrees (176 degrees Celsius) and roast the lamb bones on a cooking sheet for about 45 minutes.

2. The instant pot is set to sauté function, heat 2 tbsp olive oil, crackle cumin seeds and fenugreek seeds. Add onions, crushed garlic, ginger, jalapeño peppers

3. Sauté for 2-3 minutes or until onions become translucent. Add all the spices (cayenne, cumin, turmeric, coriander, cloves, bay leaves, and pepper powder) and sauté for another 2-3 minutes so the spices are blended well and sufficiently roasted (make sure not to burn the spices).

4. Add all the roasted bones and vegetables. Add enough water to cover all the vegetables and bones. Add vinegar.

5. Close the lid. Set the instant pot on manual setting – high-pressure and 12-hour timer.

6. Once the bones and vegetables are cooked, strain the broth into a large bowl

7. Add salt to taste, add some chopped fresh herbs of your choice and serve warm.

8. Refrigerate any remaining broth

BONE BROTH (LAMB BONES ROASTED)

Ingredients

- 3 lb lamb bones with marrow
- 1 large onion peeled quartered
- 3 medium tomatoes chopped
- 2 carrots washed cut into 1 inch long pieces
- 2 celery stalks washed and cut into 1 inch pieces
- 1 inch ginger grated
- 3-4 garlic cloves peeled and crushed
- 2-3 tbsp apple cider vinegar
- 2 tsp thyme
- ½ cup cilantro
- ¼ cup rosemary
- 1 gallon of water
- salt and pepper to taste

Method

1. Set oven to 350 degrees (176 degrees Celsius) and roast the lamb bones on a cooking sheet for about 45 minutes.

2. Add all roasted bones and vegetables and other ingredients (except vinegar salt and pepper) into an instant pot and add water and vinegar

3. Set the instant pot in manual mode, select low pressure and cooking time of 12 hrs.

4. After 12 hours, strain the broth into a large bowl. Add salt and pepper to taste. Add some fresh herbs of your choice (optional) and enjoy.

5. Refrigerate any remaining broth

CHAPTER 8. SOUPS

Making soup instant pot is, once again, an easy proposition with one button soup setting or using manual pressure cooker mode. The typical cooking time is about 20-30 minutes depending on the ingredients used.

BLACK BEAN SOUP

Black beans are rich in protein and are one of the healthiest of the beans/lentils family. Black beans have anti-cancer properties among other benefits.

Ingredients:

- 2 cups black beans – soaked in water overnight
- 1 bay leaf
- 3-4 garlic cloves peeled
- ½ medium red onion chopped
- 1 large tomato chopped
- ½ tsp pepper powder
- 1 tsp turmeric
- 1 tsp red pepper flakes
- 1 tsp cumin seeds
- ½ green or red bell pepper chopped
- 1 stick of celery cut
- 1 jalapeño (optional)
- 2-3 tsp taco seasoning
- 1 bunch cilantro

Method

1. The instant pot is set to sauté function, heat 2 tbsp olive oil, add cumin seeds, let it crackle. Add garlic,

bay leaf, Jalapeño, ginger, onion, mix well for 1-2 minutes
2. Add turmeric, paprika, pepper powder. Sauté for another 2-3 minutes
3. Add celery, bell pepper, and celery. Mix well so the vegetables are coated with the spice mixture. Add the desired amount of water, vegetable broth, chicken broth, or bone broth.
4. Close lid and cook on beans function
5. Release the steam naturally.
6. Open the lid and add the finely chopped cilantro. Add salt to taste and enjoy warm.

LENTIL SOUP

Lentils are rich in protein and like the black bean soup from the previous recipe; the lentil soup below provides a wholesome meal especially when you are sick or recovering from sickness. These can be enjoyed as a regular meal otherwise also and is a good option when trying to eat less/lose weight and still want a nutritious meal.

Ingredients:

- 2 cups of dry lentils (any color)
- 3-4 garlic cloves peeled
- 1 medium red onion chopped
- 3 medium tomato chopped
- ½ tsp pepper powder
- 1 tsp turmeric
- ½ tsp paprika
- 1 tsp cumin seeds
- ½ green or red bell pepper
- 1 stick of celery chopped
- 1 jalapeño (optional)
- 1 tsp dried basil
- 1 bay leaf
- 1 bunch cilantro chopped
- 8 cups water/vegetable broth/chicken broth/bone broth from one of the broth recipes.
- 2 tsp olive oil

Method

1. The instant pot is set to sauté function, heat 2 tbsp olive oil, add cumin seeds, let it crackle. Add garlic,

bay leaf, Jalapeño, ginger, onion, mix well for 1-2 minutes

2. Add turmeric, paprika, and pepper powder. Sauté for another 2-3 minutes
3. Add tomatoes, bell pepper, and celery. Mix well so the vegetables are coated with the spice mixture. Add the desired amount of water, vegetable broth, chicken broth or bone broth.
4. Close lid and cook on beans function
5. Release the steam naturally.
6. Open the lid and add the finely chopped cilantro. Add salt to taste and enjoy warm.

SPICY TOMATO SOUP

Ingredients:

- 4-6 tomatoes chopped
- 3-4 garlic cloves peeled
- 1 inch ginger grated
- 1 medium red onion chopped
- ½ tsp pepper powder
- 1 tsp turmeric
- ½ tsp paprika
- 1 tsp cumin seeds
- 1 bunch cilantro chopped
- 8 cups water/vegetable broth/chicken broth/bone broth from one of the broth recipes.
- 2 tsp olive oil

Method

1. The instant pot is set to sauté function, heat olive oil, add cumin seeds, let it crackle. Add garlic, Jalapeño, ginger, onion, mix well for 1-2 minutes

2. Add turmeric, paprika, pepper powder. Saute for another 2-3 minutes
3. Add tomatoes and mix. Add the desired amount of water, vegetable broth, chicken, or bone broth.
4. Close lid and select manual setting, high pressure 5 minutes.
5. Release the steam naturally.
6. Use a blender to puree the soup until smooth and creamy. Add chopped cilantro and salt to taste. Enjoy warm.

SPICY CREAM OF BROCCOLI AND KALE SOUP

Broccoli and Kale are considered superfoods. Combine it with ginger, garlic, and turmeric – some of the best spices and some herbs and we get a healthy and nutritious soup.

Ingredients:

- 4 cups of broccoli florets
- 2 cup of kale chopped
- 3-4 garlic cloves peeled
- 1 inch ginger peeled and chopped
- 1 medium red onion chopped
- ½ tsp pepper powder
- 1 tsp turmeric
- ½ tsp paprika
- 1 tsp cumin seeds
- 1 stick of celery chopped
- 1 jalapeño (optional)
- 1 tsp dried basil
- 1 bay leaf
- 1 bunch cilantro chopped

- 8 cups water/vegetable broth/chicken broth/bone broth from one of the broth recipes.
- 2 tsp olive oil

Method

1. The instant pot is set to sauté function, heat 2 tbsp olive oil, add cumin seeds, let it crackle. Add garlic, bay leaf, Jalapeño, ginger, onion, mix well for 1-2 minutes
2. Add turmeric, paprika, pepper powder. Sauté for another 2-3 minutes
3. Add celery, broccoli, and kale and mix well so the vegetables are coated with the spice mixture. Add the desired amount of water, vegetable broth, chicken broth or bone broth.
4. Close lid and cook on soup function
5. Release the steam naturally.
6. Transfer the soup into a blender. Add more water/broth if needed. Blend until smooth
7. Return the soup from the blender into the one pot. Close the lid and set it for low pressure and 5 minutes of timer. Add chopped cilantro, salt to taste.

BUTTERNUT SQUASH SOUP WITH LENTILS

Ingredients:

- 4 cups of butternut squash peeled and cut into 1 inch pieces
- 3-4 garlic cloves peeled
- 1 inch ginger peeled and chopped
- 1 medium red onion chopped
- ½ tsp pepper powder
- 1 tsp turmeric
- ½ tsp paprika
- 1 tsp cumin seeds
- ¼ cup split pigeon peas washed
- 1 jalapeño (optional)
- 1 bunch cilantro chopped
- 4 cups water/vegetable broth/chicken broth/bone broth from one of the broth recipes.
- 2 tsp olive oil
- Salt to taste
- 1 tsp lemon juice (optional)

Method
1. The instant pot is set to saute function, heat 2 tbsp olive oil, add cumin seeds, let it crackle. Add garlic Jalapeño, ginger, onion, mix well for 1-2 minutes until onions turn translucent.
2. Add turmeric, paprika, pepper powder. Saute for another 2-3 minutes
3. Add lentil and butternut squash. Add the desired amount of water, vegetable broth, chicken broth or bone broth.
4. Close lid and cook on manual mode – high pressure, 30 minutes.

5. Release the steam naturally.
6. Open lid, Transfer the soup into a blender. Pulse it a few times so the soup is smooth.
7. add cilantro, and salt (to taste). Add optional lemon juice.

CHICKEN AND VEGETABLE SOUP

Ingredients:

- 1 chopped up chicken breast
- ½ cup chopped up carrots
- ¼ cup green peas
- ½ cup chopped up broccoli florets
- ½ cup potatoes cut into small cubes
- 2 medium tomatoes
- 3-4 garlic cloves peeled and chopped
- 1 inch ginger grated
- 1 medium red onion chopped
- 1 jalapeno
- ½ tsp pepper powder
- 1 tsp turmeric
- ½ tsp paprika
- 1 tsp cumin seeds
- 1 bay leaf
- 1 bunch cilantro chopped
- 8 cups water/vegetable broth/chicken broth/bone broth from one of the broth recipes.
- 2 tsp olive oil

Method

1. The instant pot is set to saute function, heat olive oil, add cumin seeds, let it crackle. Add garlic, Jalapeño,

ginger, onion, bay leaves, and mix well for 1-2 minutes

2. Add turmeric, paprika, and pepper powder. Sauté for another 2-3 minutes or until spices become fragrant.
3. Add chicken, tomatoes and other vegetables. Mix well for a couple of minutes. Add the desired amount of water, vegetable broth, chicken, or bone broth.
4. Close lid and select manual setting, high pressure 8 minutes.
5. Release the steam naturally.
6. Open lid. Add salt and cilantro. Mix well and serve.

DISCLAIMER

This book details the author's personal experiences in using Indian spices and information contained in public domain as well as the author's opinion. The author is not licensed as a doctor, nutritionist or chef. The author is providing this book and its contents on an "as is" basis and makes no representations or warranties of any kind with respect to this book or its contents. The author disclaims all such representations and warranties, including for example warranties of merchantability and educational or medical advice for a particular purpose. In addition, the author does not represent or warrant that the information accessible via this book is accurate, complete or current. The statements made about products and services have not been evaluated by US FDA or any equivalent organization in other countries.

The author will not be liable for damages arising out of or in connection with the use of this book or the information contained within. This is a comprehensive limitation of liability that applies to all damages of any kind, including (without limitation) compensatory; direct, indirect or consequential damages; loss of data, income or profit; loss of or damage to property and claims of third parties. It is understood that this book is not intended as a substitute for consultation with a licensed medical or a culinary professional. Before starting any lifestyle changes, it is recommended that you consult a licensed professional to ensure that you are doing what's best for your situation. The use of this book implies your acceptance of this disclaimer.

Thank You

If you enjoyed this book or found it useful, I would greatly appreciate if you could post a short review on Amazon. I read all the reviews and your feedback will help me to make this book even better. For your convenience, please click the following link to take you directly to Amazon where you can post the review.

APPENDIX I: INSTANT POT COOKING TIMES

Cooking Time Tables
12 PSI
HIGH PRESSURE LEVEL

VEGETABLES

ASPARAGUS	BEANS (yellow & green)	BROCCOLI (florets)	BRUSSELS SPROUTS	BUTTERNUT SQUASH
1-2 mins	1-2 mins	1-2 mins	2-3 mins	4-6 mins
CABBAGE (whole or wedges)	CARROTS (whole or chunks)	CAULIFLOWER (florets)	CORN (on the cob)	MIXED VEGETABLES
2-3 mins	6-8 mins	2-3 mins	3-5 mins	3-4 mins
POTATOES (large, whole)	POTATOES (small, whole)	POTATOES (cubed)	SWEET POTATOES (whole)	SWEET POTATOES (cubed)
12-15 mins	8-10 mins	3-4 mins	12-15 mins	2-4 mins

MEAT & EGGS

BEEF (stew)	BEEF (large pieces)	BEEF (ribs)	CHICKEN (breasts)	CHICKEN (whole)
20 mins (per 450 g / 1 lb)	20-25 mins (per 450 g / 1 lb)	20-25 mins (per 450 g / 1 lb)	6-8 mins (per 450 g / 1 lb)	8 mins (per 450 g / 1 lb)
CHICKEN (bone stock)	LAMB (leg)	PORK (butt roast)	PORK (baby back ribs)	EGGS (large)
40-50 mins	15 mins (per 450 g / 1 lb)	15 mins (per 450 g / 1 lb)	15-20 mins (per 450 g / 1 lb)	Hard: 5 mins

www.instantpot.com/instantpot-cooking-time

Instant Pot

RICE & GRAINS (grain : water ratio)

BARLEY (pearl)	CONGEE	MILLET	OATMEAL	OATS (steel cut)	PORRIDGE
20~22 mins 1:2.5	15~20 mins 1:4~1:5	10~12 mins 1:1.75	2~3 mins 1:2	3~5 mins 2:3	5~7 mins 1:6~1:7

QUINOA	RICE (Basmati)	RICE (brown)	RICE (Jasmine)	RICE (white)	RICE (wild)
1 min 1:1.25	4 mins 1:1	20~22 mins 1:1	4 mins 1:1	4 mins 1:1	20~25 mins 1:2

BEANS & LENTILS (dry & soaked)

BLACK BEANS	BLACK EYED PEAS	CHICKPEAS	KIDNEY BEANS (red)	KIDNEY BEANS (white)	LENTILS (green)
D: 20~25 mins S: 6~8 mins	D: 14~18 mins S: 4~5 mins	D: 35~40 mins S: 10~15 mins	D: 20~25 mins S: 7~8 mins	D: 25~30 mins S: 6~9 mins	D: 8~10 mins S: N/A

LENTILS (yellow)	LIMA BEANS	NAVY BEANS	PIGEON PEAS (gandules)	PINTO BEANS	SOYBEANS
D: 1~2 mins S: N/A	D: 12~14 mins S: 6~10 mins	D: 20~25 mins S: 7~8 mins	D: 25~30 mins S: 6~9 mins	D: 25~30 mins S: 6~9 mins	D: 35~45 mins S: 18~20 mins

SEAFOOD

FISH (whole)	FISH (fillet)	LOBSTER	MUSSELS	SHRIMP (or prawn)	SEAFOOD STOCK
4~5 mins	2~3 mins	2~3 mins	1~2 mins	1~3 mins	7~8 mins

PREVIEW OF OTHER BOOKS IN THIS SERIES

ESSENTIAL SPICES AND HERBS: TURMERIC

Turmeric is truly a wonder spice. It has anti-inflammatory, anti-oxidant, anti-cancer, and anti-bacterial properties. Find out the amazing benefits of turmeric. Includes many recipes for incorporating turmeric in your daily life.

Turmeric is a spice known to man for thousands of years and has been used for cooking, food preservation, and as a natural remedy for common ailments. This book explains:

- Many health benefits of turmeric including fighting cancer, inflammation, and pain.
- Turmeric as beauty treatments - turmeric masks
- Recipes for teas, smoothies and dishes
- References and links to a number of research studies on the effectiveness of turmeric

Essential Spices and Herbs: Turmeric is a quick read and offers a lot of concise information. A great tool to have in your alternative therapies and healthy lifestyle toolbox!

PREVENTING CANCER

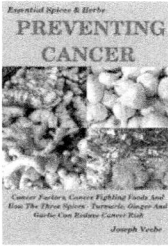 World Health Organization (WHO) estimates more than half of all cancer incidents are preventable.

Cancer is one of the most fearsome diseases to strike mankind. There has been much research into both conventional and alternative therapies for different kinds of cancers. Different cancers require different treatment options and offer a different prognosis. While there has been significant progress in recent times in cancer research towards a cure, there are none available currently. However, more than half of all cancers are likely preventable through modifications in lifestyle and diet.

Preventing Cancer offers a quick insight into cancer-causing factors, foods that fight cancer, and how the three spices, turmeric, ginger and garlic, can not only spice up your food but potentially make all your food into cancer fighting meals. While there are many other herbs and spices that help fight cancer, these three spices work together and complementarily. In addition, the medicinal value of these spices has been proven over thousands of years of use. The book includes:

- Cancer-causing factors and how to avoid them
- Top 12 cancer-fighting foods, the cancers they fight and how to incorporate them into your diet

- Cancer-fighting properties of turmeric, ginger and garlic
- Over 30 recipes including teas, smoothies and other dishes that incorporate these spices
- References and links to many research studies on the effectiveness of these spices.

PREVENTING ALZHEIMER'S

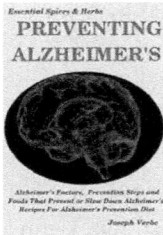

Approximately 50 million people suffer from Alzheimer's worldwide. In the U.S. alone, 5.5 million people have Alzheimer's – about 10 percent of the worldwide Alzheimer's population.

Alzheimer's disease is a progressive brain disorder that damages and eventually destroys brain cells, leading to memory loss, changes in thinking, and other brain functions. While the rate of progressive decline in brain function is slow at the onset, it gets worse with time and age. Brain function decline accelerates, and brain cells eventually die over time. While there has been significant research done to find a cure, currently there is no cure available.

Alzheimer's incidence rate in the U.S. and other western countries is significantly higher than that of the countries in the developing world. Factors such as lifestyle, diet, physical and mental activity, and social engagement play a part in the development and progression of Alzheimer's

In most cases, if you are above the age of 50, plaques and tangles associated with Alzheimer's may have already started forming in your brain. At the age of 65, you have a 10% chance of Alzheimer's and at age 80, the chances are about 50%.

With lifestyle changes, proper diet and exercise (of the mind and body), Alzheimer's is preventable.

In recent times, Alzheimer's is beginning to reach epidemic proportions. The cost of Alzheimer's to the US economy is expected to cross a trillion dollars in 10 years. It is a serious health care issue in many of the western countries as the population age and the life expectancy increase.

At this time, our understanding of what causes Alzheimer's and the ways to treat it is at its infancy. However, we know the factors that affect Alzheimer's and we can use that knowledge to prevent, delay the onset or at least slow down the rate of progression of the disease.

While this book does not present all the answers, it is an attempt to examines the factors affecting Alzheimer's and how to reduce the risk of developing Alzheimer's. A combination of diet and both mental and physical exercise is believed to help in prevention or reducing risk. The book includes:

Discussion on factors in Alzheimer's development

The list of foods that help protect the brain and boost brain health is included in the book:

Over 30 recipes including teas, smoothies, broths, and other dishes that incorporate brain-boosting foods:

References and links to several research studies on Alzheimer's and brain foods.

ALL NATURAL WELLNESS DRINKS

It contains 35 recipes for wellness drinks that include teas, smoothies, soups, and vegan & bone broths. The recipes in this book are unique and combine superfoods, medicinal spices, and herbs. These drinks are anti-cancer, anti-diabetic, ant-aging, heart healthy, anti-inflammatory, and anti-oxidant as well as promote weight loss.

By infusing nature-based nutrients (super fruits and vegetables, spices, and herbs) into drink recipes, we get some amazing wellness drinks that not only replace water loss but nourish the body with vitamins, essential metals, anti-oxidants, and many other nutrients. These drinks may be further enhanced by incorporating spices and herbs along with other superfoods. These drinks not only help heal the body but also enhance the immune system to help prevent many forms of diseases. These drinks may also help rejuvenate the body and delay the aging process. The book also includes suggested wellness drinks for common ailments.

ESSENTIAL SPICES AND HERBS: GINGER

Ginger is a spice known to man for thousands of years and has been used for cooking and as a natural remedy for common ailments. Recent studies have shown that ginger has anti-cancer, anti-inflammatory, and anti-oxidant properties. Ginger helps in reducing muscle pain and is an excellent remedy for nausea. Ginger promotes a healthy digestive system. The book details:

- Many health benefits of ginger including fighting cancer, inflammation, pain and nausea
- Remedies using ginger
- Recipes for teas, smoothies, and other dishes
- References and links to a number of research studies on the effectiveness of ginger

ESSENTIAL SPICES AND HERBS: GARLIC

Garlic is one of the worlds healthiest foods. It helps in maintaining a healthy heart, an excellent remedy for common inflections and has both anti-oxidant and anti-inflammatory properties. It is an excellent food supplement that provides some key vitamins and minerals. This book details the benefits of garlic and describes many easy recipes for incorporating garlic into the diet:

- Many health benefits of garlic including fighting cancer, inflammation, heart health and more
- Remedies using garlic
- Recipes for teas, smoothies, and other dishes
- References and links to a number of research studies on the effectiveness of garlic

ESSENTIAL SPICES AND HERBS: CINNAMON

Cinnamon is an essential spice. It has Anti-diabetic, anti-inflammatory, anti-oxidant, anti-cancer and anti-infections and neuroprotective properties. Cinnamon is a spice known to man for thousands of years and has been used for food preservation, baking, cooking, and as a natural remedy for common ailments. Recent studies have shown that cinnamon has important medicinal properties. This book explains:

- Many health benefits of cinnamon including anti-diabetic, neuroprotective and others.
- Recipes for teas, smoothies, and other dishes
- References and links to a number of research studies on the effectiveness of cinnamon

ANTI-CANCER CURRIES

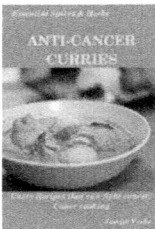

It is estimated that more than 50% of the cancer incidents are preventable by changing lifestyles, controlling or avoiding cancer-causing factors, or simply eating healthy. There are several foods that are known to have anti-cancer properties either directly or indirectly. Some of these have properties that inhibit cancer cell growth while others have anti-oxidant and anti-inflammatory properties that contribute to overall health. However, many spices and herbs have direct anti-cancer properties and when one uses anti-cancer spices and herbs in cooking fresh food, there is an immense benefit to be gained. Curry dishes are cooked using many spices that have anti-oxidant, anti-inflammatory, and anti-cancer properties.

This book contains 30 curry recipes that use healthy and anti-cancer ingredients. These recipes are simple and take an average of 20-30 minutes to prepare.

BEGINNERS GUIDE TO COOKING WITH SPICES

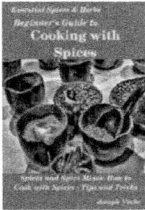 Have you ever wondered how to cook with spices? Learn about the many benefits of spices and how to cook with them!

Find out how to start using spices as seasoning and healthy foods. Includes sample recipes,

Beginner's guide to cooking with spices is an introductory book that explains the history, various uses, and their medicinal properties and health benefits. The book details how they may be easily incorporated in everyday cooking. The book will cover the following:

- Health benefits of spices and herbs
- Spice mixes from around the world and their uses
- Tips for cooking with Spices
- Cooking Vegan with Spices
- Cooking Meat and Fish with spices

- Spiced Rice Dishes
- Spicy Soups and Broths

EASY INDIAN INSTANT POT COOKBOOK

Instant Pot or Electric Pressure Cooker is the most important cooking device in my kitchen. It saves me time, energy, and helps me prepare hassle-free Indian meals all the time.

The Easy Indian Instant Pot Meals contains includes:
- Recipes for 50 Indian dishes
- Tips for cooking with Instant Pot or any electric pressure cooker
- General tips for cooking with spices

FIGHTING THE VIRUS: HOW TO BOOST YOUR BODY'S IMMUNE RESPONSE AND FIGHT VIRUS NATURALLY

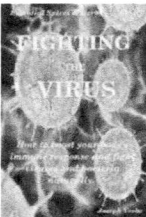

What can we do to improve our health and immune response so that our bodies are less prone to viral or bacterial infections? How can we enable our body for a speedy recovery in case of getting such infections?

The answer lies in lifestyle changes that include better hygiene

practices, exercise, sleep, and a better diet to keep our body in optimum health. This book is focused on understanding the body's immune system, factors that improve the body's immune response and some natural remedies and recipes. The book contains:
•Overview of the human immune system
•Factors affecting immune response
•Natural substances that fight viral, fungal and bacterial infections
•Recipes that may improve immunity and help speedy recovery
•Supplements that may help improve the immune system
•Scientific studies and references

EASY SPICY EGGS: ALL NATURAL EASY AND SPICY EGG RECIPES

 Recipes in this book are not a collection of authentic dishes, but a spicy version of chicken recipes that are easy to make and 100% healthy and flavorful. Ingredients used are mostly natural without any preserved or processed foods.

Most of these recipes include tips and tricks to vary and adapt to your taste of spice level or make with some of the ingredients you like other than the prescribed ingredients in the recipes.

There are about 30 recipes in the book with ideas to make another 30 or even more with the suggestions and notes included with many of the recipes. Cooking does not have to be prescriptive but can be creative. I invite you to try your own variations and apply your creativity to cook dishes that are truly your own.

FOOD FOR THE BRAIN

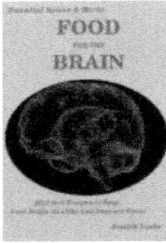

Nature provides for foods that nourish both the body and the brain. Most often the focus of the diet is physical nourishment, - muscle building, weight loss, energy, athletic performance, and many others. Similar to foods that help the body, there are many foods that help the brain, improve memory and help slow down the aging process. While it is normal to have your physical and mental abilities somewhat slow down with age, diseases such as Alzheimer's, and Parkinson's impact these declines even more. Brain function decline accelerates, and more and more brain cells eventually die over time.

With regular exercises, strength training, practicing martial arts and other physical activities can arrest the physical decline. This book's primary focus is on managing decline in mental and brain function through diet and contains the following:
Characteristics of foods that helps in keeping your brain healthy and young. Brain healthy foods including meats, fruits, vegetables, spices, herbs, and seafood. Supplements to improve memory, cognition and support brain health
Mediterranean diet recipe ideas
DASH diet recipe ideas
Asian diet recipe ideas
Brain boosting supplements and recommendations products and dosage
References

Printed in Great Britain
by Amazon

60461607R10068